MESSIAH

SAINT JULIAN PRESS

POETRY

Praise for MESSIAH

Anne Babson's *Messiah* takes an energetic leap of faith into sound and spirit. This is the Bible on acid, King James' cadence meets a jazzy barbaric yawp that is distinctly American. Babson knows her way around the testaments—old and new—and insists the stories they contain are relevant for our times. She invites us to "Live powerfully, strongly kneeling, singing!" Reader, be you heathen or believer, you may find yourself saying *Amen.*

—Grace Bauer
Author of *The Women At The Well* and *MEAN/TIME*

Anne Babson's *Messiah* begins in the throes of a storm, then picks up velocity poem by poem. These lines roar with the truth, as if delivered from the lips of an Old Testament prophet who's seen the sins of this modern world. There are wars here, economic peril, political corruption, drug abuse, environmental demise, everything society has wrought in this world. There is also the clarity of a poet who's reckoned these things so clearly, they've burned a path for us toward redemption. These poems sing, they growl, they hiss, and they re-envision history and future in ways necessary to redemption today.

—Jack B. Bedell
Poet Laureate, State of Louisiana, 2017-2019

Anne Babson's *MESSIAH* is heady, whirling, and nothing short of ecstatic. It is a must read for fans of poetry who wish to be utterly transported.

—Maurice Carlos Ruffin
Author of *We Cast a Shadow: A Novel*

MESSIAH

Poems

by

Anne Babson

SAINT JULIAN PRESS
HOUSTON

Published by
SAINT JULIAN PRESS, Inc.
2053 Cortlandt, Suite 200
Houston, Texas 77008

www.saintjulianpress.com

COPYRIGHT © 2019
TWO THOUSAND AND NINETEEN
©Anne Babson

ISBN-13: 978-1-7320542-7-1
ISBN: 1-7320542-7-4
Library of Congress Control Number: 2019941090

Cover Art Photography: Anne Babson & Ron Starbuck
Cover Design: Ron Starbuck

To YH.

MESSIAH

"A voice of noise from the city, a voice from the temple, a voice of the Lord that rendereth recompence to his enemies." — Isaiah 66:6

CONTENTS

New Orleans Quintet	1
Comfort Ye	4
Every Valley Shall Be Exalted	6
And the Glory of the Lord: Legato Arrangement	9
The Threshing Floor	10
Recitative: Thus Saith the Lord	12
Thus Saith the Lord (Transposed for Soprano)	13
But Who	14
And He Shall Purify	15
Behold, A Virgin Shall Conceive	16
Good Tidings to Zion	17
Darkness Shall Cover the Earth	19
The People that Walked in Darkness	20
The Rich Young Ruler	21
Pifa (Pastoral Symphony)	22
Chorus: Glory To God	24
Rejoice Greatly	25
From a Scroll Found at Nag Haamadi	27
Then Shall The Eyes of the Blind	28
His Yoke is Easy	30
He Was Despised	32
Surely He Hath Borne Our Griefs	33
And With His Stripes We Are Healed	34
All We Like Sheep Have Gone Astray	35
He Trusted in God	36
Behold, And See if There Be Any Sorrow	37
He Was Cut Off	38
Gnostic Scroll	39
Air: But Thou Didst Not Leave His Soul in Hell	40
Chorus: Their Sound is Gone Out	41
Recitative: Unto Which of the Angels	42
Chorus: Let All the Angels of God Worship Him	43
Air: Thou Art Gone Up on High	44
Chorus: The Lord Gave the Word	45
Chorus: Hallelujah	48
Since By Man Came Death	53
Recitative: Behold, I Tell You A Mystery	56
Air: The Trumpet Shall Sound	57

Recitative: Then Shall Be Brought to Pass	59
But Thanks Be to God	60
If God Be For Us	61
In Thanks for Mary	62
Worthy Is the Lamb That Was Slain	68
Amen	70

MESSIAH

MESSIAH   Anne Babson

NEW ORLEANS QUINTET

I.

I saw my city sliding in sludge.
Cockroaches cowered in corners and courts.
Bridges and barges bore barnacled bludgeons.
Shotguns and shipyards shared circuit shorts.

Where my flag boy? Where my flag boy?
My visitation — when? Who dat?

I beheld buildings bolted shut burnt.
Criminals crawled out crying like crows.
Bakers bought bad flour, buggy and turnt.
Officers offered offal and oaths.

Who my big chief? When my big chief?
Where dat — one stone left on other?

II.

I loaded it with big–four rhythms, my ark.
I loaded it with those lazy lipped singers,
Whose every eighth note drags its foot just so,
    Moan moans like my lover just woke low,
      Just jelly–rolled over, stretched and hummed.

I basted the beams with molasses and mud.
I coated them with hickory and candy corn.
I paired the dancers together, two by two.
    Threw beads, restocked bourbon, closed the trap.
    We are crouching here in the deluge dark.

The sky is clear now, but just you wait!
Storm's a coming! We are battened.
    We are slattern. We are patterned.
    We are fattened calves. We are mutton.
    We are battened down. We are batter.
    Hey, batter! Hey, batter, batter!

Where my flag boy? Where my flag boy?
My visitation — when? Who dat?
Who my big chief? When my big chief?
Where dat — one stone left on other?

MESSIAH   Anne Babson

III.

Beloved Christmas–only attendees,
won't grasp this Ash Wednesday passage's
    Raw form: "All flesh is as grass…All
        The glory of man as the grass flower."

Here's how you'll understand it – scatted:
        Flesh grass fatted. Glory glass gassed.
        Flower flesh flattened. Man gas flower.
        Grass, gas, or ass – no one rides for free.

Now y'all see, all y'all? Let us pray.
You own that bumper sticker. Amen.

> *Where my flag boy? Where my flag boy?*
> *My visitation — when? Who dat?*
> *Who my big chief? When my big chief?*
> *Where dat — one stone left on other?*

IV.

When I returned, my wet roads churned like lava.
The earth stank — demon pigs drowned in Galilee.
I yanked up broken boards. They melted in my hands —
    Paper pulp, paper flowers for the dead, *flores para los muertos*.
    My gloves, clasped together penitentially, were bulldozers.

And the worst was, I wasn't even quite arrived there yet.
I am having this great preservation premonition in reverse.

I watched a woman lying in the avenue.
Her friends were screaming, looking up.
    She clutched her wet belly, heard sirens.
    Only then I shouted, "Get down! He's armed!"

We all knew he was armed. They're all armed.
    This is America, isn't it? We have the right.
My prophecies just don't astonish.
    They happened years ago. They happen again.

> *Where my flag boy? Where my flag boy?*
> *My visitation — when? Who dat?*
> *Who my big chief? When my big chief?*
> *Where dat — one stone left on other?*

MESSIAH   Anne Babson

V.

I saw a city sliding in sludge.
Criminals crawled out crying like crows.
Shotguns and shipyards shared circuit shorts.
Officers offered offal and oaths.
    It's that season again — we mask, pretend
    Sin is original, but we have sinned again.

Where my big chief? Where messiah?
Where the good news? Where the blues?
Where the bastions? Where the beads?
Where the bones? Where the bile?
Where beatitude? Where the bog?
Yes, the bog — the bog that selects,
The threshing floor, the Darwin?

I am poured out like water. The tide rises.
I predict this has happened before.
I look back; this will happen again.

Where my flag boy? Where my flag boy?
My visitation — when? Who dat?
Who my big chief? When my big chief?

MESSIAH   Anne Babson

COMFORT YE

"Comfort ye, comfort ye my people, saith your God. Speak ye comfortably to Jerusalem and cry unto her, that her warfare is accomplished, that her iniquity is pardoned." — Isaiah 40 1–3

Coo to the bombed–out buildings, stroke, comfort
Them. Shake the bandaged hands gashed in warfare,
Not by chopping wood in the wilderness.
Make contact with blood–shot eyes, then prepare
Them for another bombshell. Run there. Speak
Clearly through the megaphone, say *"Desert*

"Your hopelessness, urban snipers! Desert
All fallout shelters and even comfort
Zones! Drop your gas masks! The Better Way speaks,
So now hear this: Your bitterness, warfare,
And tangled tunnels end here, today! Prepare
For new explosions in the wilderness.

"These ones don't blow apart the wilderness
Survivalists; they turn the cracked desert
Clods to a champagne fountain, y'all! Prepare
For new bombardments, these of pies, comfort
Foods, and new shoes just your size! The warfare
Is over, I promise y'all!" Hurry. Speak

To the maimed ones. Tell the mutes they will speak.
Tell dead park lawns they will sprout wilderness.
Tell the dog–faced marine vets the warfare
Will turn into an all–night rave, desserts
Will burst out of artillery, comfort
Treacle instead of mortar shells, prepared

Snack foods from grenade launchers. Go. Prepare
The city's worst neighborhoods. When you speak,
Make sure they know you're not a cop. Comfort
The orphans, crack whores, the mob, the wilderness
Lunatics strewn homeless in deserted
Box cars, amassed amputees of warfare

Past, tell them, *"Go AWOL from this warfare;*
I draft y'all for new battle. Help prepare
The new highway through the corpse–strewn desert,
Demolishing only ghost towns. Help speak
Peace to friends, foes in methed–out wilderness.

MESSIAH   Anne Babson

Help pave the way for their rescue, comfort,

And, above all else, their truest dessert,
Not the one they've earned in the long warfare,
The one I give forgiving: my comfort."

MESSIAH   Anne Babson

EVERY VALLEY SHALL BE EXALTED

"Every valley shall be exalted, and every mountain and hill shall be made low: and the crooked shall be made straight, and the rough places plain:" — Isaiah 40:4

New Jersey, your comatose cul–de–sacs
                        will be exalted!
Your monoxide–spewing Turnpike
                        will snake crooked!
Your rubber–tire strewn marshlands
                        will blossom exalted!
Yes, your toxic waste dumps
                        will rise green, exalted!
Basement apartments in Camden,
                        rented through crooked
Real Estate with no repairs
                        will turn penthouse, exalted!
The cots of the warehouse night watchmen:
                        King–size! Exalted!
      Your uphill southern logging roads
                        will uncurl downhill straight!
The unkempt Newark ghetto football fields
                        will be mowed straight!
Armpit state of the stinky Northeast,
                        be wash–clothed, be exalted!
Yes, oh state–wide chemical blight beyond
                        the fruited plain,
Your hour has finally arrived on its white
                        thoroughbred — plain

Dust shoots from hooves; snakes dart
                        Medusa slithers into plain
Potholes at the sound of such Hi–ho–Silver,
                        William–Tell–exalted–
Overture thunder. Yes, your hour has come,
                        your hero a plain–
Clothes officer of the reckoning, armored in white
                        HASMAT, plain–
Spoken, broom–wielding, a holy janitor is
                        your champion, exalted
As a Bruce Springsteen chorus repeated on
                        the radio, as plain
As a Jersey twang–tuned ballad to his beloved,
                        if dirt–plain,
Jersey girls perming their already over–processed

MESSIAH   Anne Babson

                            hair crooked,
Gluing on the lids of their dull, murky eyes
                                false and crooked
Lashes, adding no fire to their desperately lean,
                            pink, plain
Pavonia–Newport Mall–shoplifted, bottle–blonde,
                            über–straight
Girl looks looking for hair–gelled, sneakered,
                                muscled straight

Boys at Hoboken hot spots, where, New Jersey,
                            your straight
Couples couple, the beer–goggles blurring purple
                            all the plain
Failures —flabby guts, buck teeth and adult
                                braces, straight–
Up ugly pug noses on Rutgers grads, and
                                the hair holes straight
Men spray paint over with infomercial–
                            snake–oiled plain
Brown shoe polish. These mean meetings
                            lead to straight
Copulation in parked cars with Jersey plates,
                            some straight,
Double–barreled shotgun weddings, these
                            occasionally exalted
By white picket fence without end, amen,
                                despite all, exalted
Like you are, New Jersey, you smelly floozy,
                            in this straight–
Talking story, despite the facts: most meetings
                            end crookedly
In promises unkept to phone next week,
                            in syrupy, crooked

Flattery followed by an unending,
                            pregnant, crooked
Silence, yet New Jersey, land of Love Canal,
                            I say straight
Will be leveled, and repaved, and retarred
                            all your crooked
Back alleys of factory towns, smoothed
                            all your crooked,
Secret footpaths leading to Jimmy Hoffa's
                            shallow, straight,

MESSIAH

Anne Babson

Unmarked grave, and forgiven will be
                          all your crooked
Boss–politicking days with your
                          arthritis–gnarled, crooked
Hands held out hungrily for government
                          graft in plain
Sight. This will not deprive you of
                          dumb luck, plain
Grace unfurled over your rotten,
                          Body–odiferous, crooked
Philandering, pandering, slandering ways.
                          Be exalted!
Be the Garden State! Yes, despite yourself,
                          most exalted!

The crooked, frozen reeds over Mafia hits
                          shall be made straight.
The abandoned shale quarries crawling
                          with rats made plain,
And the sewage swamps, oh,
                          the stench made rosy, exalted!

MESSIAH Anne Babson

AND THE GLORY OF THE LORD: LEGATO ARRANGEMENT

"And the glory of the LORD shall be revealed, and all flesh shall see it together: for the mouth of the LORD hath spoken it." — Isaiah 40:5

It squats in bud form, bound up darkly. It waits
In its shell, roasted, ready to be cracked.
The egg, the start of all feathered things, lies
Inert, undistinguished, barely warm, the same
Shape as a zero filled in, ready to pop.
It is on its way.

It is on its way. In the age of the microwave,
One forgets the watched pot never boils. The
Bubbles will rise as soon as He sabers the cork.

It is on its way. Hallowed ground stinks of dung.
Don't be fooled by acrid air. That's the smell of
First strawberries fixing to sprout up ripened.

It is on its way. She's not getting chubby.
That's not a sign of any couch–potato sloth.
She is great with child. Yes, child, she is great.

MESSIAH — Anne Babson

THE THRESHING FLOOR

Rich men's bastards, high yellow as wheat, munch crumbs
(With lard lumps) scraped off the plantation threshing floor.
       My head rests on a rock pillow on the sorghum field.

       I watch archangels swarm like termites from star to star.
"Planes," Styron tells me and points toward the army airbase.
      Not plain, not planes, not planets, granites, but grocers

      Stocking the shelves bustle the night inventory,
Storing borage, shelving bevels on the threshing floor.

We woke, returned to America. How it had changed!
      The A & P turned to Alpha and Omega.
       We see three dozen bean brands

       preening like prom queens,
Matches match matchlessly to light wise virgins' lamps.
    Under florescent, halogen haloes the saints.

      Oh! Bar–coded abundance! New Jerusalem!
        New and Improved Jerusalem, now with menthol!
Ginsberg, Whitman and I cruise the aisles seeking souls.

    The big box night clerk points outside, warns us,
"Check the garden center. We got them on order.
Right now none left, but maybe on the threshing floor."

What will we serve guests at the Twelve Oaks barbecue?
    "Not proper for a lady to show her bosom
       Before three," has written the many–breasted God.

And what will I write? Will I tighten the corset
    Or scream from unbridled guts the Jeremiad?

      The Yankees are coming! The Yankees are coming!
      Hide mee–maw's silver cups under the threshing floor!

Chaff and wheat murmur goodbye at the Greyhound stop.
    One rolls in the grinder, transfigured to biscuits.
      The other ends up as pig poop, methane, vapor.
        After revolution, emancipation, boom,
It's still Big Daddy's house, cousins worked as lackeys.
You think the swamp fever hitting them won't get in?

MESSIAH	Anne Babson

      The germ warfare we practice infects us as well!
           Big Daddy and that nevermore raven stalk
                 Gothic hallways as Poe ghosts. Power grids go out.

              Turn the ignition. Illuminate truck headlights.
They crook white reaper fingers toward the threshing floor.

MESSIAH   Anne Babson

RECITATIVE: THUS SAITH THE LORD

He goes up to the booth,
Taps on glass. The bored clerk
      Takes out her ear buds,
      Glares at him. She leans
      Forward reluctantly,

Grabs the microphone,
And it crackles when
      She asks, "What?" He slips
      The Metrocard through the
      Change socket and asks
Her to test it for
The available
      Amount. "Taste and see."
      "Is it broken?" She
      Asks. He shakes his head a

And smiles. The card glows,
Flashes at her the
Annual earnings
Of the whole world.
      "This can't be right," She

Gasps, but it is right.
She knows it is right.
He smiles at her like
Her BFF, laughs,
      "Quit. Come with me. Let's

Unlock the turnstile
      For all humankind
      On that lost line where
      They paved over the
      Entrances and steps."
She puts the "Out of
Service" sign in front
Of the window, grabs
Her jacket, and they
Catch the Bronx–bound A.

MESSIAH   Anne Babson

THUS SAITH THE LORD (TRANSPOSED FOR SOPRANO)

"For thus saith the Lord of hosts: yet once,
It is a little while, and I will shake..."
                      She closed her Bible with its gilded front,
                      Then opened it again, a double take:
"The heavens, and the earth...the sea...the land;
And I will shake all nations, and the desire
Of all nations shall come" under His hand?
                      Under our brick gothic revival spire?
Where? *"and I will fill this house with glory."*
                      Which house? cathedrals? Or the synagogues?
                      Which house? My house? Could it be my body,
                      This torso, the temple of the living God?
She thought of her breasts in a white light flood.
The sermon moved on. The prophesy stood.

BUT WHO

"But who may abide the day of his coming? and who shall stand when he appeareth? for he is like a refiner's fire..." — Malachi 3:2

At the bank, we get taught by the expert: deadliest catches abide
Until the nibble. Then, we receive the second lesson: the Refiner's
Rotisserie perfects the trout in olive oil. We are bold to say: appear

Again, oh, hungered–for *icthus*! Come back! We pray reappear
Tonight! For so very long in your love we have yearned yet abide,
And now the tractor–sower overtakes the combine reaper; the Refiner

Makes way for the speeding miner's cart. Yes, the smiling Refiner
Staggers under the weight of so many new nuggets appearing
Out of each new shaft blown open. We beseech you, abiding,

Stay awake with us this hour. We abide, for the Refiner's
Campfire will warm our hands until you once again appear.

MESSIAH   Anne Babson

AND HE SHALL PURIFY

"and he shall sit as a refiner and purifier of silver: and he shall purify the sons of Levi, and purge them as gold and silver, that they may offer unto the Lord an offering in righteousness." — Malachi 3:3

       We are urns balanced so
       Ably by the palms of
This ceramicist that
       In this kiln heat we will
       Not shatter we will not
Melt away we will not
       Burn to crisp frieze fragments
       Even when it hurts like hell
Just to listen for Him
As we wait for the door
       To open again and
To look Him once again
In the majestic eye.

MESSIAH   Anne Babson

BEHOLD, A VIRGIN SHALL CONCEIVE

"Therefore the Lord himself shall give you a sign; Behold, a virgin shall conceive, and bear a son, and shall call his name Immanuel." — Isaiah 7:14

"Behold, a virgin shall be with child, and shall bring forth a son, and they shall call his name Emmanuel, which being interpreted is, God with us." — Matthew 1:23

A rough shift this evening, darlin'! I worked graveyard again.
This girl came in. Was she even fourteen? Pregnant.
She claimed she had never done a dang thing that would
Get a girl in trouble. She barely knew about
Birds and bees. So young, sweet really! I told her all
Her options. She's keeping it. She says she has a
Boyfriend who'll help out – so she hopes. Thank God
Parental notification isn't required
In this state! She thinks her father already knows.
I bet he does, the bastard! What those girls go through!
Sure didn't come from the right side of the tracks, but
She had this air about her, kind of elegant.
Nothing I said scared her. They most times cry.
She was – how can I explain it – expecting joy.

MESSIAH   Anne Babson

GOOD TIDINGS TO ZION

"O Zion, that bringest good tidings, get thee up into the high mountain; O Jerusalem, that bringest good tidings, lift up thy voice with strength; lift it up, be not afraid; say unto the cities of Judah, Behold your God!" — Isaiah 40:9

"Arise, shine; for thy light is come, and the glory of the Lord is risen upon thee." — Isaiah 60:1

Oh, artists bringing beauty to gang turf,
        transcend conventions of your black–clad scene.
Oh, optimists defying the zeitgeist,
        go South to the survivalists' campgrounds.

        Breathe fresh air above their stuffy bunkers.
Oh, majestic mercy missionaries,
Call the press conference.
    Take the mike.
        Clear your throat.
            Tap.
                Ask if this thing is on.

Despite their tense, quizzical expressions,
        declare to all the broadcast journalists,
Proclaim to the combat photographers,
    "Point the camera this way to film God!"

        "Pan the camera this way to film God!"
Declare to all the broadcast journalists,
        "Zoom the camera this way to film God!"
Oh, artists bringing beauty to slum streets,

Your masterpiece trembles in your brushes.
        The light bulbs above your heads flash on now.
    The first refrain occurs to you at last.
He who paints you on this world's canvas,

Who composes your music in the spheres
  has deigned to breathe craft into your fingers,
        Has deigned to sing through your impudent mouths.
He who paints you on world canvas,

Who sculpts your flesh out of estuary mud,
    who bangs out your hearts' percussion solos
        Has deigned to sing through your impudent mouths.

MESSIAH
Anne Babson

Oh, artists bringing beauty to offramps,

Oh, majestic mercy missionaries,
Oh, optimists defying the zeitgeist,
Oh, artists bringing beauty to ghettoes,
                the light bulbs above your heads flash on now.

Your masterpiece trembles in your brushes.
        Declare to all the broadcast journalists,
                "Point the camera this way to film God!"
        Aim the camera this way to film God,

He who paints you on this world's canvas,
oh, artists bringing beauty to strip malls!
        Your masterpiece trembles in your brushes.
                Zoom the camera this way to film God.

He who paints you on this world's canvas,
        who composes your music in the spheres,
Bangs out your hearts' percussion solos,
        has deigned to sing through your impudent mouths.

MESSIAH   Anne Babson

DARKNESS SHALL COVER THE EARTH

"For, behold, the darkness shall cover the earth, and gross darkness the people: but the LORD shall arise upon thee, and his glory shall be seen upon thee. And the Gentiles shall come to thy light, and kings to the brightness of thy rising." — Isaiah 60: 2–3

The child, the one in the corner, sings something surprising.
Her music teacher listens for the brightness of her rising.

Willie has few teeth left and weeps in this session, but his
Addiction concluded. Now watch the rightness of his rising.

Djeme escaped the man who beat her, spoke no English, but
Now she learns in college all the slightness of her rising.

Juan cleaned toilets for six years until the green card, but look –
His own business now, all due to the pridelessness of his rising.

The fog stood over the hills all morning like a crock pot lid.
Now it curls back a grin. Blue greets the whiteness of its rising.

Nights along the Hudson watch the moon above the Bronx
Beckon all pleasure cruisers to float guideless at its rising.

When we found her, she was too weak to stand, but now
Slowly she comes to her feet – the lightness of her rising!

The company fired May just before she was vested in options.
The stock goes up now. She watches spiteless at its rising.

The dictator planned his life in palaces, but the population
Took up arms. He shakes his fists, mightless at its rising.

I won't give up on these poems. I will rewrite them. They will
Soar yet. I tell you, listen for the tightness of Anne's rising.

MESSIAH   Anne Babson

THE PEOPLE THAT WALKED IN DARKNESS

"The people that walked in darkness have seen a great light." — Isaiah 9:2

The pushers primping in the shadowed alleyways,
The hookers cooking in the lethal lean–to flats,
The disaffected after–schoolers in their haze,

The ancient hermit ladies with their many cats
Have all seen the flashpoint open like a white bloom,
Have all heard the new composition's chords and strats.

The laid–off day laborers in their lonely room
Have all shivered suddenly as the breeze broke fresh
Over awful actuaries adding in gloom,

Over Evel Kenevels leaping snakes and flesh,
Over oval arenas filled with blood sport fans,
Over underachievers caught in complex mesh.

They have all seen the new, wonderful bridge's spans.
They have all seen the cantilevers' festooning,
Cleavaging, coiling, bowing, minuetting trance.

They have all, despite their old fears, dreamed of crossing
Out of their place of slavishness into free work
Out of their hovel's whoredom, boredom into things

Invigorating, sparking oil fires from this murk,
Igniting light that lasts in this loaded, lead lair,
Shattering black holes apart with a shrieking jerk.

Out of the fetid dankness into tasty air,
Out of the algae seepage into the running stream
The clarity has hit them with light to spare.

They scrape out of the scraps into the creamy cream.
They break out of brackets into the holy whole.
They shake out of shackles into the dreamy dream.

The light liberates the consciousness–raising cold
That wakes zombies zealously out of their death daze
And makes pig iron alchemically turn to gold.

MESSIAH   Anne Babson

THE RICH YOUNG RULER

After his meeting with that rabbi, he
Walked home more slowly than usually.
His two valets kept quiet at his side.
He looked over his shoulder, once, twice but
Did not turn around. He would not do it.
What fool would do such a thing, in his place?
He wondered why he could not laugh at it.
He sighed, "Another charlatan," and yet —
Back home, the servant knelt at his feet, poured
Water in silver, unhooked his sandals.
His mother, at her embroidery, asked
The answer that man gave to his question.
He said nothing, just watched the needle flash
As she threaded its narrow eye once more.

MESSIAH   Anne Babson

PIFA (PASTORAL SYMPHONY)

Eternity spots us in the wilds of North America
Where the poets ice fish for new similes in the snow,
Where the plains crinkle under the feet of Bison
Like sheets of the poets' paper in the Winnebego,
Where they try to translate the meter of the moose
And make a couplet out of the white weasel's rustle.

Eternity begs a dance of us. Her sloping skirts rustle
The routes where the plows lift her early American
Petticoats for a peek. Out for a nibble, the moose
Take a nip at the grass. Her wink melts the snow
In patches, and the poets, in their rocking Winnebego
Take notes for the next works to be banned in Bison,

Wyoming's public library for eternity. The real bison,
The ones snorting in their wool, in disapproval rustle
As they nip at sparse greenery around the Winnebego's
Wheels. The poets dully exclaim, "Now this is America!"
And they contemplate making naked angels in the snow
Until they open the door and see the shuddering moose

In this eternal sub–zero weather, realize their own moose
Parts, unleathery, are too delicate to mingle with the bison
In the shifting drifts of the many textures of tangoing snow.
The poets know the Eskimo coined hundreds of names to rustle
For it, but speaking only the current tongue of North America,
They only know one name for it but a slew for their Winnebego.

Eternity laughs at her minion poets in their rickety Winnebego
That will one day be rust under the hooves of her mighty moose.
Eternity is content to whirl her skirts around the ugly Americans
Of pretty winter words and wait with the incredibly patient bison
For the day when they retake the prairie together. She rustles
An encouraging word in their hairy ears. She whispers snow's

Myriad names, a code for the overarching, eternal power of snow
Blindness, which afflicts all the paper–chasers in the Winnebego,
Who grasp nothing but the tomes of verse sheets which they rustle
In a white oblivion. They speak neither Eskimo dialects, nor moose
Modern, nor the cries of the worried hawk, nor the bellows of bison.
They only speak the nasal post–industrial twangs of North America,

MESSIAH
Anne Babson

So what, Eternity whispers to
                the noplussed, constant bison in a lusty rustle,
Can the blind poets hope in the clunky American–assembled Winnebego
To know of her schemes,
    or their dead–pan jokes,
        or of the plans of moose?

MESSIAH   Anne Babson

CHORUS: GLORY TO GOD

"And suddenly there was with the angel a multitude of the heavenly host praising God, and saying, Glory to God in the highest, and on earth peace, good will toward men." — Luke 2:13–14

Shoo doop m' doo
     Shoo doop m' doobie doo
Shoo doop m' doo
     Shoo doop m'doobie doo
   dip dip dip dip   dip dip dip dip dip
 Dip dip dip dip   dip dip dip dip dip
Staples and glue,
Eraser rubber stamp,   *Glory to the Handler's Hands*
Marshmallows, too,   *Out–juggling the craftiest*
Mint leaves and lava lamp!   *Acrobats.*

Zebra and gnu,   *Glory to the Way of ways*
Goose, duck–billed platypus,   *Out–weighing the weightiest*
Snow caribou,   *Waiters.*
No snuffaluffagus!

         Glory to the Mind of Minds
Cure for the flu,   *Outsmarting the smartest*
Mending of broken toe,   *Smarty–pants.*
Missing limbs grew,
Leprosy has to go,   *Glory to the Chiefs of Chiefs*
         Out–seeing the seamiest
Jade, turquoise blue,   *CEOs.*
Peridot, garnet red,
Black pearls to chew,   *Glory to the Word of words*
An emerald for your bed!   *Out–speaking the speakeasy*
         Speakers.
Hot chicken stew,
Your momma's chocolate cake, *Glory to the Light of lights*
With ice cream, too,   *Out–beaming the bulimic*
Peppercorn sirloin steak!   *Beamers.*

Room with a view,
In marble pantheon,   *Glory to the Voice of Voices*
Upholstered new,   *We re–echo His echo's*
Soft lights, soft music on!   *Echoes.*
oooooo– oooooooooooo! oooooo– oooooo–   Ooooo !

MESSIAH   Anne Babson

REJOICE GREATLY

"Rejoice greatly, O daughter of Zion; shout, O daughter of Jerusalem: behold, thy King cometh unto thee…lowly, and riding upon an ass, and upon a colt the foal of an ass." — Zechariah 9:9–10

      Rise up you Detroit daughters, shake skirts! shout!
            Despite the tension in the streets, rejoice!
      Your booty shaking leads to hooting shouts
      From the sons of Motown, soprano shouts
            From the Motor City's aunts, *"Rejoice,*
    But keep the noise down!" but no matter, shouts
      From fishes in Lake Michigan, and shouts
For the end of the sedan's dominion
And the cookie–cutter car's dominion,
      For the end of the fender bender, shout,
The end of *Pax Cadillaca*, the peace
Of the luxury car, replaced by peace

Of the pipe smoked by Pontiac, the peace
      Of the plain warriors no longer shouting
For Custer but wishing his daughters peace
And the grandsons of the pioneer peace
      On their absconded land taken with shouts
Of manifest destiny from peaceful,
Rightful owners who now wish the thieves peace,
      Who generously with these crooks rejoice,
      Who with white, pitchfork–tongued farmers rejoice
Wishing their combines and harvesters peace
Despite the injustice made dominion,
Despite the automotive dominion,

The from–car–to–shining–car dominion,
The automatic–versus–clutch–war's peace.
Detroit daughters, claim your own dominion,
Over General Motors, dominion
That delivers to the union reps peace
That ends *maquilladora* dominion
And gives the auto worker dominion
      Over the machine with a victor's shout
      And pay–raise. Oh, daughters of Detroit, shout
Yourselves a new fief, a new dominion
         Over your own lives at last – oh, rejoice,
         Daughters of the new Michigan, rejoice

         For industrial blight beknighted. Rejoice!

MESSIAH
Anne Babson

For ending streamlined dominion,
        Low-riding design uplifted, rejoice!
        For the new wheels-to-shining-wheels, rejoice!

Here it comes — souped-up, ridden in dominion,
        For His swerve-turning to the right, rejoice!
        For His jump-thumping to the left, rejoice!
For the signal of your low-riding peace
King parallel parking in perfect peace,
        Spinning, spinning His custom rims, rejoice!
        Oh, daughters of Detroit, get in and shout!
        For the convertible converted, shout!

Know that your king, *El Rey Pacifico*,
Of the low riders comes in dominion
To pick you up for a slamming, pimped-out joyride,
    Oh, desired daughters of motor city, so shout!

MESSIAH   Anne Babson

FROM A SCROLL FOUND AT NAG HAAMADI

Oh, daughter of Zion, oh, daughter of Jerusalem,
I can never deliver this prophesy. I have come
To tell you to rejoice, and rejoice abundantly you

Will, but I, the prophet, will return to my cave alone
Without you, oh, favored of the One who speaks behind me!
Oh, daughter of Zion, oh, daughter of Jerusalem,

If only mine were the voice in the Song of Solomon
Beckoning you to me, but you are not my comely one.
I stand before you and proclaim my Great Rival's message,

Oh, but daughter of a land in which I am mad man,
Daughter of a walled city in which I am a tourist,
There are forbidden words I would speak to you if I did

Not serve One who feeds me with ravens, whose Voice Itself
Is my foremost drink, who would make that fountain a dry bed
If I used my coal–sterilized mouth to run over your

Sun–sanctified skin, if my tongue, tool carving prophesy,
Slipped in crooks of your elbows, curves of your back, the
Cavern of your ear, the caves where Essenes never venture.

Oh, daughter of Zion, oh, daughter of Jerusalem,
My wild, undeclared words sear my lips now. Servants cannot
Deliver any but the Master's gifts. Forgive me my

Silence on the questions you dare to ask me in silence.
Forgive me my speaking another language to you than the
One most urgent to me. Forgive me most that I do not

Rejoice with you, wise virgin awaiting your bride groom with
Well–oiled lamp. Although if were you the betrothed of any
Other I would elope with you tonight, I will not come.

MESSIAH — Anne Babson

THEN SHALL THE EYES OF THE BLIND

"Then the eyes of the blind shall be opened, and the ears of the deaf shall be unstopped. Then shall the lame man leap as an hart, and the tongue of the dumb sing: for in the wilderness shall waters break out, and streams in the desert." — Isaiah 35:5–6

Then shall be opened the eyes of the blind.
    Rubes trusting state government shall spot graft.
    Crones gone antiquing shall find the lost craft.
Contracts will be read before they are signed.
Unctuous beauties shall get ogled streamlined.
    Dour dowagers will be caught in mid–laugh.
Then shall be opened the eyes of the blind.
    Rubes trusting state government shall spot graft.
Loose–goose floozies shall get caught in a bind.
    High–five–ing high rollers shall lose a half.
    Poop deck swabbers shall be caught in the aft.
Devil–may–care call girls shall see and shall mind.
Then shall be opened the eyes of the blind.

Then shall the ears of the deaf be unstopped.
    The truth shall be heard despite all the lies.
    Children will quit playing *Lord of the Flies*
To listen to the ocean floor get mopped.
Retirees unshod will sing songs sock–hopped,
    Crouch to hearken to the floor pipe's sighs.
Then shall the ears of the deaf be unstopped.
    The truth shall be heard despite all the lies.
Show tunes shall echo from plays long since flopped
    And questions reverberate – "Who?"s, "What?"s "Why?"s
    A Grand Canyon resonance for the wise,
A radio silence for fools' words chopped,
Then shall the ears of the deaf be unstopped.

Then shall the lame person leap as a hart.
    The proud knee shall buckle with gratitude.
    The shop clerks will lose the snide attitude,
And the traffic cop shall direct as art.
Then shall the aisle cruisers mosh at Walmart.
    Airline pilots shall loop with latitude.
Then shall the lame person leap as an hart.
    The proud knee shall buckle with gratitude.
The golfers shall cartwheel out of their carts.
    The professors shall all ply their platitudes.
    The curmudgeons all shift their shattered moods.

MESSIAH   Anne Babson

Then shall the zombie awake with a start.
Then shall the lame person leap as a hart.

MESSIAH   Anne Babson

HIS YOKE IS EASY

"For my yoke is easy, and my burden is light." — Matthew 11:30

Gnostic proverbs from
Solomon King of Leonia,
New Jersey, taught to him by his mother:

To breathe in this suburban air is hard.
                               To choke is easy.
Recognize the used car salesman in your midst and run.
                               His joke is easy.

Opera is not for the anti–intellectual, but, though twangy,
                               folk is easy.
The FDA inspector's riddle – Mad cow in lard, know
                               the yolk is queasy.

You can take Pepsi home to mother, but the bathroom wall says
                               Coke is easy.
Power Ball is tricky; Horatio Alger, impossible. Bill Gates, please!
                               Broke is easy.

The laundress hears Wisdom Herself murmur the secret –
Spin cycles toil.
                               To soak is easy.
The unicycle teeters under the clown, but on the lone wheel
                               the spoke is easy.

To the slothful man, the fire in the belly is inscrutable, but the resulting
                               smoke is easy.
Neanderthal fire–building is revealed at last. To spark is labor.
                               To stoke is easy.

"Dude!" shouts the fool misquoting Gershwin, "It's summertime, and
                               the toke is easy."
Casanova's last words: "To tickle, *fratello mio*, is an art, but
                               to poke is easy."

"No!" replies Captain Kangaroo contrarily, "Pokey's hard, but
                               Hokey's easy."
"Both wrong!" adds the grammarian, "'Awakened,' is hard, but
                               'awoke' is easy."

So notes the wise barrista: half–caff–half–latte grande is hard.

MESSIAH

Anne Babson

Mocha is easy.
The devil is in the white, observes the short order cook, but
the yolk is easy.
To the Italian grandmother, daughters–in–law are hard, but
gnocchi are easy.

The first shall be last and the last first. The willow is hard, and
the oak is easy.

HE WAS DESPISED

"He is despised and rejected of men; a man of sorrows and acquainted with grief: and we hid as it were our faces from him; he was despised, and we esteemed him not." — Isaiah 53:3

Methods have changed, but the motives stand
As permanently as the Curse. Only blood washes
Away the mats of hair, the charred remains of it.
Then, the howling, a DNA–anchored cyclone, loops
And loops unto third and fourth generations, and it
Passes away only with that same blood's washing
And rewashing. Madly you have thought yourself
Unimplicated in the executioner's job description
Listed in the want ads section of *The Lubbock Bugle*.
You thought yourself exonerated, but those levers
Release poisons hydraulically to make everybody
Woozy. Drunk, you hear its voice cry unto me from
The ground. Despite your protests, you don't regret
What you have done to rid the world of such scum.

MESSIAH   Anne Babson

SURELY HE HATH BORNE OUR GRIEFS

"Surely he hath borne our griefs and carried our sorrows: yet we did esteem him stricken, smitten of God, and afflicted." — Isaiah 53:4

The things that once were only mine to shoulder surely
Have been picked up by another porter, one who bears
A muck of luggage – disasters, losses, bruises, griefs,
Shadows, embarrassments — all willingly, ably carried
Upstairs to rooms with southern exposures, no sorrows.
I search through my purse for a good enough tip, and yet
What can I hand from this sack that conveys any esteem?
So uplifted, I see my spiny Pandora's boxes have stricken
The gentleman kind enough to carry packages, have smitten
The mittens that grip the handles and pull them along. God
Knows why he would do this for me, let himself be afflicted
With the blemishes, lice and acidic burns stemming most surely
From my own lack of moral hygiene! Who would agree to bear
My burdens, the rusty rolled–up pains stuffed in the folded griefs?

MESSIAH — Anne Babson

AND WITH HIS STRIPES WE ARE HEALED

"But he was wounded for our transgressions, he was bruised for our iniquities: the chastisement of our peace was upon him; and with his stripes we are healed." — Isaiah 53:5

In cancer wards, where tubes string out Alaska Pipelines pumping
Vital signs out of wizened women, where nurses check marks and
Doctors have learned not to care about anyone in the rows of beds
So that when death comes, it does not take M.D.s with its new quarry,
And the toxins come in capsules or beams as needed, and fear eyes
Gape to shadow demons waiting, waiting, waiting their turn to gnaw
The gowned ones raw, there, even at the eleventh hour, He comes.
Though they will explain it away with Latin terms and the latest
Armamentarium articles double–blind, remission is spiritual. One
Won't see him in textbooks, but He shrinks tumors as He blinks,
Waves fingers and draws stinking corpses out vivid once more,
And with His stripes — scars bearing balm druggists upholding sponges
Dipped in vinegar and myrrh to mock and numb will always deny –
And with His stripes, taken one by one as prescribed, we are healed.

MESSIAH   Anne Babson

ALL WE LIKE SHEEP HAVE GONE ASTRAY

"All we like sheep have gone astray; we have turned everyone to his own way; and the Lord hath laid on him the iniquity of us all." — Isaiah 53:6

In Golden Gate Park, during the Summer of Love — if one
Calls brief, anonymous hook-ups in the weeds that unfathered
Children it fathered anything like love – all the wild things
Danced blithely, an errant swarm of saffron-ash-spangled
Monarch butterflies headed for the Mexican forest of their
Perpetual mating migration caught in an unseasonable storm
That blew them off course into bay currents to grounds
Where witchery, drugged orgies, and promising musicians
Who overdosed young on the excesses of that gilded hour
All scattered in Pacific wind like lost tie-dyed bandanas.
The astrologers claimed it was predestined, a new age
Dawning with collateral damage borne of past hypocrisies,
Which to be sure, provoked them sorely, but, misbegotten ones,
The real post-Woodstock cleanup crew is a one-man show.

HE TRUSTED IN GOD

"He trusted on the Lord that he would deliver him: let him deliver him, seeing he delighted in him."
— Psalm 22: 8

This was the note they found in the box with the escape artist's remains:

"Dear fans,

I know this looks grim. In fact, what could look worse?

I have scribbled this note using my own blood and the tip of my
Shoelace. I only have a few minutes of oxygen left, so let me
Explain my plan: You probably thought this stunt would end
With my escape from the box like I did that time when the
Sponsors of this event tried to throw me off a cliff in Nazareth.

This is not in fact the stunt I have called you here to witness.
This one will take me longer than the three hours set aside by
The sponsors today, but this will be the ultimate escape of all time.
No one has ever done it before – an escape not from a hellish
Peril but from Hell itself. What's more, I will not only escape
From that prison – I'll wriggle out with all the people stuck there
Who are willing to come with me through the same escape hatch.
I will leave the hatch open for all future users who remain part
Of my fan club's lifetime membership database. This will be great!

Thanks for watching. Keep looking for updates posted on
www.fishersofmen.net

Your pal,"

The management regrets this unfortunate incident. Clearly,
He went mad right before the end. Obtain refunds
At the box office, or patrons may use their ticket stubs for
Future events, subject to availability.

MESSIAH   Anne Babson

BEHOLD AND SEE IF THERE BE ANY SORROW

"Is it nothing to you, all ye that pass by? behold, and see if there be any sorrow like unto my sorrow, which is done unto me." — Lamentations 1:12

I am banging my head against the blue chintz–
Papered wall as the baby chomps at my breast.
With the paring knife, I am cutting my fingers
Shallowly as I score the meat where I will salt it.
In the supermarket, people roll their carts by me
As I am weeping into frozen peas. In the bathroom,
I am holding myself around my middle but can
Not seem to vomit or even dry heave it out of me.
I leave them with the TV but am exiting in seconds.
What good mother ever leaves the room for more
Than a minute? That's how accidents are occurring.
I am seeing the toddler through thick glass brick
Without focusing on his gestures. They are reminding
Me of ripples on a tar–black pond emanating from
Catfish feeding off the bottom. I am ripping hairs
From my head one by one as that chenille–draped
Dinosaur sings again. I am chewing my thumbnails,
Then Super–gluing on French–manicured plastic ones.
I am burning myself with the corner of the new iron.
It leaves me ice–packing a new dimple, a tear, a rune.
I am painting my face shades of pink before you get home.
I am kissing you hello as if I were still someone you knew.
Your shirts are pressed, rugs vacuumed; dinner is ready –
Brisket and scalloped potatoes, just as you like them.
The children's faces are washed, hair smooth. The news
Is on in the next room. Bad things are happening today –
Floods, earthquakes, fires, shootings, rapes, but not to you.

HE WAS CUT OFF

"He was taken from prison and from judgment: and who shall declare his generation? for he was cut off out of the land of the living: for the transgression of my people was he stricken." — Isaiah 53:8

My feet have grooved a furrow into this slab of concrete
A yard wide, three yards long, paced out over and over.
Food slides under my door, liquids through a hole. They
Know me by number, but no one calls my name in its true
Authority. When I come into my kingdom, I will remember
The guards who whisper apologies, ask about their future,
Their worries. I forgive everyone. This keeps my gaze off
The floor. I plan my parliament. I know I receive letters,
But they do not slip them to me. I imagine what they say
And just what I respond. Back and forth I walk reciting my
Dictation to the walls — decrees, edicts, replies, complete
With punctuation for my prophesied typist to faithfully record.
Take this missive to my captors: *Gentlemen, every sentence*
Ends, and this one will conclude with an exclamation point.

GNOSTIC SCROLL — *For Amy Irvin*

In spite of it all, we have stood up to spy it.
We spied the mad farmer mourn soybean crops rotting.
We spied broken bridges and cars falling off them.
We spied a black bullet etched with a code number.
We spied a PT boat dry docked and dry roasted.
We spied the lost preacher adrift on an iceberg.
We spied the barbed wire encircling charred cacti.
We spied hatchet ladies on stools breaking glasses.
We spied lonesome men smoking blunts in bleak alleys.
And who are we, who are we to ask the whirlwind why?

In spite of it all, we have screamed and spat at it.
We spat at smug bakers with Caucasian icing.
We spat at the sparrers in boxing shorts pounding.
We spat at spokesmodels and at the bright gaslights.
We spat at the gamblers devouring our nickels.
We spat at bad beadles who pilfer from pockets.
We spat at spin doctors with wires in their wingtips.
We spat at the school bus that rides to the prison.
And who are we, who are we to ask the whirlwind why?

In spite of it all, we have stared it down darkly.
We stared down the ravens that croak out the doomsday.
We stared down the canyons that shadow bright rivers.
We stared down the skiers on slopes quickly melting.
We stared down the porch chimes that ring without reason.
We stared down the bankers that bet on bad augurs.
We stared down the dealers dispensing down death–quilts.
We stared down the dollar stores stocking salt coffins.
And who are we, who are we to ask the whirlwind why?

Out of the whirlwind whoosh wonderous misfits.
Out of the whirlwind ricochets riffing.
Out of the whirlwind fling folktales and riddles.
Out of the whirlwind bursts blossoming folly.
Out of the whirlwind howls grace and howls mercy,
Forgive us, Big Chief, for counsel so darkened.
Forgive us, Big Chief, for words without knowledge.
Forgive us, Big Chief, for this, our America.
Behold, we are vile. What can we, oh, what can we answer?

MESSIAH   Anne Babson

AIR: BUT THOU DIDST NOT LEAVE HIS SOUL IN HELL

"For thou wilt not leave my soul in hell; neither wilt thou suffer thine Holy One to see corruption." — Psalm 16:10

PCBs on the
Muddy bed of the Hudson
Lift out. The shad feed.

Lake Placid's acid
Rain pockmarks stones, then oddly
Disappears. Where? How?

Strip–mined Nevada
Mountains turn woody again
Overnight – jackpot!

The prairie overtakes old
Cornfields presaged only by
Crop circles Thursday.

The sequoia trees
Thicken like chest hair on a
Californian teen.

The Mississippi
Morning mist clears revealing
Drinkable water.

Birds, beasts, plants, insects
Diversify their holdings
In America.

Redemption looks like
A tree frog laying eggs in
The pitch–sticky swamp.

MESSIAH — Anne Babson

CHORUS: THEIR SOUND IS GONE OUT

"But I say, have they not heard? Yes verily, their sound went into all the earth, and their words unto the ends of the world." — Romans 10:18

The older woman rock star tongues
The younger woman rock star's buns.
Their sound goes into all the Earth,
We flip the channel; it is done.

The football murderer in white
Range Rover floors it in his flight.
His sound goes into all the Earth,
He lands in handcuffs that same night.

Candidates' hats tossed in the ring,
One says a stupid, racist thing.
His sound goes into all the Earth,
And it vanishes in polling.

Twelve men, some women, travel fast
To tell one story. It is passed.
Its sound goes into all the Earth,
And for two thousand years it lasts.

MESSIAH   Anne Babson

RECITATIVE: UNTO WHICH OF THE ANGELS SAID HE AT ANY TIME

"For unto which of the angels said he at any time, Thou art my Son, this day have I begotten thee? And again, I will be to him a Father, and he shall be to me a Son?" — *Hebrews 1:5*

DNA,
How do you
Know how to
Shape my nose
With all the
Cosmetic
Surgeons who
Stalk me with
Scalpels in
Their sweaty,
Bill–clenching,
Practiced fists?
With all the
Thigh Masters
On the shelves
Of K–Mart,
How do you
Remember
My mother's
Jutting hips?
In which of
The members
Of the cast
Of *Charlie's
Angels* have
You remained
Unaltered?
I strike my
Action pose
Silhouette,
Defending my
God–given,
Abundant
Derriere.

MESSIAH   Anne Babson

CHORUS: LET ALL THE ANGELS OF GOD WORSHIP HIM

"he saith, let all the angels of God worship him." — Hebrews 1:6

Bell
        Doo–wah, doo–wah!   *This one goes out to all the cherubim and seraphim*
Bell   *To Gabriel and his trumpeters, and the whole host*
        Doo–wah, doo–wah!   *Of Heaven. From the one and only biggest–bopping*
Bell   *Big Bopper. Happy holiday! Take it, boys!*
Let all the angels worship Him!

Bell   *The sodium sticky in the salt–lick, slick down!*
        Doo–wah, doo–wah!   *The uranium ugly in the green dark, park down!*
Bell   *The iron hardy in the ship yard, slip down!*
        Doo–wah, doo–wah!   *The helium squealy in the big tank, spank down!*
Let all the elements worship Him!

Bell   *The wind withering in the wuthering, whisper down!*
        Doo–wah, doo–wah!   *The rain reigning in the stadium. crane down!*
Bell   *The hail pailing at the shale quarry, wail down!*
        Doo–wah, doo–wah!   *The sleet fleecing in the wheat fields, beat down!*

Bell
        Doo–wah, doo–wah!
Let all the weather worship Him!

Bell
        Doo–wah, doo–wah!   *The mollusk cowering in the cowrie, bow down!*
Bell   *The antelope loping on the park slope, slow down!*
        Doo–wah, doo–wah!   *The skunk slinking like an old monk, hunker down!*
Bell   *The blow fish swishing in the wet wash, low down!*
Bell
        Doo–wah, doo–wah!
Let all the creatures worship Him!
Bell

        Doo–wah, doo–wah!   *The riveter in the brick house, quiver down!*
Bell   *The manager in the tack house, jack down!*
        Doo–wah, doo–wah!   *The hotelier in the smoke house, smote down!*
Let all the people worship him! Bell Shoo–di–ooo bop doo–wah!

MESSIAH Anne Babson

AIR: THOU ART GONE UP ON HIGH

"Thou hast ascended on high, thou hast led captivity captive: thou hast received gifts for men; yea, for the rebellious also, that the Lord God might dwell among them." — *Psalm 68:18*

Captivity captive is taken whole.
The leg irons of chain gang details now melt.
Pimps' pimping gets put out on sidewalks sold.
The whipped innocents now unhook the belt.
Gifts get given to the young Jimmy Deans,
To the good, bad, and ugly, to the tough
Customers, bums, to the past–curfew teens.
Gifts get given, ignite more than enough
Sparks to Light this sad planet's sacred lamp
To hold it aloft in commuting crowds,
To beam light in the tunnels to rout that
Darkness, to podcast that secret aloud:
"The scandal of the universe is this:
Grand lips are pursed to give us all a kiss."

MESSIAH   Anne Babson

CHORUS: THE LORD GAVE THE WORD

"The Lord gave the word: great was the company of those that published it." — Psalm 68:11

"And God said, Let there be light: and there was light." — Genesis 1:3

"Thy word is a lamp unto my feet, and a light unto my path." — Psalm 119:105

"In the beginning was the Word, and the Word was with God, and the Word was God." — John 1:1

He held the human's shoulders – His ancient
Incomparable face, a face that
Poets tremble to imagine much less
Describe like any old face, as if His
                                       Incomparable face! Tremble, poets!
Name were ours to call like our pet poodle's,
Not a name that shatters all barriers,
Including that of sound, and yet He has
Given us His name, and we will see Him
                                       How it shatters! Berlin Wall Jericho!
Face to face – a generous miracle
That bestows again the greatest gift given.
He held the human's shoulders – both male and
Female He created them – beautiful
                                       Oh, beautiful, beautiful, beautiful!
Face to inanimate face, and in a
Gesture more tender than any kiss, He
Gave forever to us what matters most,
That makes us more than clay, that makes us more
                                       More tender than any kiss, His gesture!
Than wriggling spermatozoids yet eyeless,
That makes us more than a pile of organs
Gathered in a heap of meat over bone,
That makes us other than green mantis
                                       More than organs, bones, so much more!
That prays silently on the mossy wall,
That elevates us above the snorting
Water buffalo wallowing in marsh,
That takes us up trees unvisited by
                                       More than a natural kiss, than water!
Orange orangutans in tall forests.

MESSIAH

Anne Babson

With a gentle puff into our nostrils,
Fragrant as an unmatchable perfume,
He breathed it shimmering into our throats
                      Oh, perfume unmatchable shimmering!
To be expelled in incense offering,
The Word.
              Himself The Word, The Word, The Word Himself!
The Word Himself,
        Himself the Word,
                A spoken being, or
                        Himself being spoken,
Him, a stone tablet,
        A scroll containing
                All his dynamite,
                      A name more
Potent than
        Nuclear winter,
            Than hell unleashed.
                    Maneuvering
Beneath a breath,
        He is received in
                Clear thought, in
                      Alphabet, the
Alpha and Omega.
            He is a notion
                Fully realized
                      Before we can
Realize a thing,
        A living water
              That never lets
                    The drinker
Thirst, and yet
        Is never wet,
              Walking on
                  Water, Himself
The Word,
        The Word
              The Word
                  Himself!

For we are His poetry composed by
The letters of the genetic codes that
Swim within our cells, and yet we are so
Much more than coded! We are sung joyfully

MESSIAH

Anne Babson

Into the atmosphere like elements
He created. We are the aria
Sung out of the darkness that he opened
In a majestic swirl of lit gas lamps.

We are the composition copied in
The notebook of the Abundant One, not
Practice homework, but drafted fearfully
And wonderfully onto the pages

Of the Non-Fiction Book. We are metric.
We soar. We bounce in our cadences full
Of surprises. We are a source of delight
To the discerning eyes that read us well.

We are literary masterpieces,
Classics set on the Gutenberg presses
Before the publication of the world,
In holy words spoken one by one.

Our neurons fire in articulated
Exclamations declared passionately.
We are a love letter written to the
Writer. We are the romance novel real!

We are uttered, shouted. We are inscribed.
We are echoed, sighed. We are autographed,
Illuminated in permanent ink in
His most distinctive, elegant longhand.

MESSIAH   Anne Babson

CHORUS: HALLELUJAH

"And I heard as it were the voice of a great multitude, and as the voice of many waters, and as the voice of mighty thunderings, saying, Alleluia: for the Lord God omnipotent reigneth." — Revelation 19:6

"And the seventh angel sounded; and there were great voices in heaven, saying, The kingdoms of this world are become the kingdoms of our Lord, and of his Christ; and he shall reign for ever and ever." — Revelation 11:15

"And he hath on his vesture and on his thigh a name written, KING OF KINGS, AND LORD OF LORDS." — Revelation 19:16

The Bangor bouncers, the Trenton tree trimmers heard it.
The Wellfleet welders, the Boise bank clerks heard it.
The Prudhoe Paratroopers, the Ashland stage hands,
They threw the file in the air. The scissors clattered.

The Montpelier pet walkers, Birmingham hired hands,
The Tulsa Musclemen and the Hilo housewives,
The Eureka speakers and the Jackson Taxmen,
They opened the gate and let the horses run loose.

The Butte beauticians, Topeka tobacconists,
Redmond cryptographers, Tombstone stenographers,
St. Paul paleontologists, Fort Worth workers,
They ripped off the polyurethane gloves and squealed.

He rules. We rule. He reigns. We reign. He rocks. We rock.

The Reno receptionists, Hope interlopers,
Milwaukee turnkeys, Ann Arbor anthologists,
Florissant florists, Chicago chicken pluckers,
They hugged the guests goodbye. They sniffed back a few tears.

Toledo repomen, Lynchburg burger–flippers
Wheeling dealers, the Minot mink ranchers heard it.
Baton Rouge boatmen, Athens Mathematicians,
They fainted, opened eyes, wandered around blinking.

Biloxi boxers, Lexington lexicographers,
The Taos taco chefs and the Denver drivers,
The Omaha orthodontists, Terre Haute poets,
They discarded the shovel. They jumped in the lake.

He rules. We rule. He reigns. We reign. He rocks. We rock.

MESSIAH   Anne Babson

The Brooklyn crooks, Philadelphia deli clerks,
The Concord cartographers, Providence provosts,
The Hartford heart surgeons, the Annapolis pollsters,
They covered their mouths, and they forgave their mothers.

The Sioux Falls suit alterers, Daytona tailors,
The Charleston harlots, Chapel Hill chaplains heard it.
The Arlington Arms dealers, the Dover gophers,
They wailed, "to the Batmobile!" They spat on the floor.

They sped down Routes 1 and 66, down the
Prairie Parkway and Adventureland Drive down old
Corn Avenue and Interstate 70, down
Kellogg Boulevard and South Lewis Avenue

He rules. We rule. He reigns. We reign. He rocks. We rock.

Down Black Stockyard Road and University Street,
Lake Drive, New Jerusalem Curve, Clinton Lane,
Across Brewery Avenue and Colgate Court,
Across Gun Beach Road and up Plaza de Armas

Up the Dalton Highway and Wiamea Way,
Across Shasta Avenue and Siskiyou Road,
Microsoft Campus Drive and around Fremont Street
Down Ninth, Fourth and First Streets, up Hondo Seco Road

Across the Alameda de las Pulgas detour,
Up Appalachian Way and Temple Boulevard,
A right at Whippoorwill Lane, at Cedar Junction,
At New Heritage Court, at Toussaint Avenue,

He rules. We rule. He reigns. We reign. He rocks. We rock.

A left at Crazy Horse Way and Cahaba Drive,
At Cherokee Street and Kissimmee Boulevard,
Along Sacajawea Curve and Dixie Lane
They went straight at Reckoning and Righteousness Streets

And at Cemetery Avenue they picked up
Hitchhikers. They drove down Lenappe and Navy Streets
They kept going at Pembroke Road, at Madison
And De Kalb, and Park, and Amsterdam Avenues,

MESSIAH   Anne Babson

And on Providence Road and Wilshire Boulevard,
And they arrived ready, if a bit out of breath,
For as it is written, we shall meet Him in Bellaire.
At the unnamed arena they had only just constructed.

He rules. We rule. He reigns. We reign. He rocks. We rock.

And with them arrived every beauty queen, every
Miss in America, Miss Bowling Ball Tahoe,
Miss Calzone October, Miss Amish Cookie Dough,
Miss Greeting Card Week, Miss Power Tool Washington,
Miss Rose Parade, Miss Teenage Plastic Packaging,
Miss Sun Tan Oil Bikini, Miss Artichoke Bliss,
And they all wore their sashes and tiaras, but
 In the place of bouquets, they all carried storm–proof
 High–beam flashlights coordinated with their ball gowns.

He rules. We rule. He reigns. We reign. He rocks. We rock.

As they checked their batteries, a bright bevy of
White–clad pizza deliverymen descended
From the sky, bearing boxes with sectioned haloes.
A gaggle of white–clad Avon ladies alit,
Toting satchels overflowing with frankincense,
A truckload of white–clad fire fighters descended,
Brandishing double–edged hatchets between their teeth,
A keystone–ful of white–clad peace officers knocked,
Brandishing sharpened plowshares and Elvis rhinestones,
An administrative assistant's fantasy
Full of white–clad international couriers
Landed asking for signatures for Dead Sea Scrolls.

He rules. We rule. He reigns. We reign. He rocks. We rock.

While these descended, this doorbell–ringing army
Of the sky in white linen, they brought out the blond,
Longhaired emcee from Woodstock, not a day older
Than he was in 1969, and he yelled
For us one more time the truest of hippie truths,
"We must be in heaven, man! We must be in heaven!"

For surely this company was not from our states,
And the penitent American roadsters cheered.

MESSIAH

Anne Babson

He rules. We rule. He reigns. We reign. He rocks. We rock.

And then out of the smoke of the glass seen darkly,
He popped a wheelie to see us all face to face.
And then, out of His aerie in the highest height,
He floored it to reunite with His family.
And then keeping the appointment jotted in blood
He rumbled in at the right hour, on the right day.
And then out of the seventh seal broken open,
He thundered in rupturing what came before Him.

He rules. We rule. He reigns. We reign. He rocks. We rock.

Appearing on the crest of the Los Angeles
Smog on a white, chromed, souped–up Harley–Davidson,
He motor–crossed in, our Magnificent Stuntman!
Emblazoned on the back of his jacket in flame
Shone a fish with quarters in its mouth and the words
KING OF KINGS, for His coronation coronates,
And the words up his white leather chaps in crimson
LORD OF LORDS, for His house holds mansions within it,
And with a most holy revving he descended
Revelation–prophesied, and in front of the
Misses, all of them, He descended dropping
The kickstand in front of Miss Artichoke Bliss,
For only she kept fresh batteries for her lamp,
Now the only one lit, and at her peau de soie
High heels, He bowed his knee, a proposal gesture.

He rules. We rule. He reigns. We reign. He rocks. We rock.

She declared, stammering, losing her spokes model
Composure momentarily, "I would rather
Be baptized by you, sir. Why do you come to me?"
And The Wildest Harley Rider told her only,
"Suffer it to be so now." Miss Artichoke Bliss
Placed her own tiara on His full head of hair,
And a lone American Bald Eagle, piercing
The hush with its plaintive, endangered cry, swooped down,
Ready to taste the flesh of evil dictators
Barbequed like the rats it chases in the Rocks,
Circled to land on His superlative shoulder,
And a voice from above thundered the commandment,
"Revolution today, then Eden tomorrow,"
And The Great Harley Rider rose again. We knelt.

MESSIAH   Anne Babson

The Earth was silent but for His footsteps, crowned as
He was, this time not with thorns but with allegiance.

He rules. We rule. He reigns. We reign. He rocks. We rock.

The age of tears, of neuroses, of breakage, of
Damage, of mismanagement, of exploiting, of
Sniveling, of groveling, of graft, of growling,
Of howling, of weeping, of creeping, of sleeping

He rules. We rule. He reigns. We reign. He rocks. We rock.

Is over forever, and now we are champions,
Now friends, now ticket holders, now frisked admitted,
Now shareholders, now valued customers, now heirs,
Now buckaroos, now Beatlemaniacs, now blessed,
Now barkeeps, now backstage groupies, now VIPs,
Now Ikettes, Now Knicks City pretty dancers, now
Slick kickstand–kicking biker chicks. No longer the
Pock–marked, we are now rockers, now rockers, now rockers
Because He rules, we rule, He reigns, we reign, He rocks, we rock.
Because we must be in heaven, man! We must be in heaven!

MESSIAH   Anne Babson

SINCE BY MAN CAME DEATH

"For since by man came death, by man came also the resurrection of the dead. For as in Adam all die, even so in Christ shall all be made alive. But every man in his own order: Christ the firstfruits; afterward they that are Christ's at his coming." — 1 Corinthians 15: 21–22

No one has ever asked me that before, but since you do:

Once the gate imploded
And the bars flew howling
Once the guns were loaded
Only to be melted yowling
Once those goaders toadied
And the plaguers placated
Begging for mercy, and gates,
Oh, I have told you that, faded
Into an ochre brimstone haze,

I moved forward. The molten
Prison bricks tumbled unfixed
From the lava walls unbolted
From the sulfur cement–mixed
Reinforcements that had held
The captives captive, had welded
The workers to the wheel, melded
The masons to the moat. The cells
Scattered and the alarm, hell's bells,

Sounded uselessly, the prison break
Was broken, and I was the crowbar
Ripping up the hinges. "Meet maker.
Be free." I gently told them all. Far
Fewer denied me than I thought would.
The Philistines circumcised their hoods.
The Amalekites tore down idol woods.
The Samaritans, released, played the *ud*.
The other tribes, hands lifted, just stood.

But I plowed through them, searching
For the very one you just mentioned.
As I strode forward, minions lurching
Begged for mercy, hunched henchmen
Screamed their bloody murders madly
But now uselessly, now to be bad badly,
Now to wreak havoc herein only sadly

MESSIAH   Anne Babson

On the ones who reject my rescue gladly.
I released yet others, ancients glad, free,

The flooded from Noah's liner cruise,
The Babel tower builders, the giants,
The East of Eden tribes now loosed,
But there was still one missing. Rants
From lesser evils petered out. At last
I found the last door, most locked fast
And guarded by the worst ones massed
Together in a huddle, a muddle clasped
Together in the darkest dark. I passed

Them. They turned to white ash smoke.
I touched the thickest door down there.
As I did to the deaf man's ears, I spoke
The word "*ephphatha*," and in a despair
It creaked slightly ajar. A howling wind
Escaped it, stale as death itself. The mind
Trapped in the gargoyle guard rescinded
Its authority over it, crying, "This old rind
Is the last morsel!" And then I entered in.

I found him bearded, covered with a fig
Leaf long since mummified, shivering,
A thick stench that would have made a pig
Run, a mottled gaze, scarred skin, quivering.
I squatted down low and lifted his chin.
"Hello, my other father," I said with a grin.
"I have come for you, if you want to begin
Again. Let's try it this time without the sin.
You and your descendants, me included, win."

He blinked at me, no doubt sure I was a new
Form of torture – there had been so many –
Or a wild dream. But understanding grew
On his face. He looked behind me for any
Demons, but I was unescorted. He tried
To speak for the first moment in an applied
Physics calculation of time. "Yes," he sighed.
I helped him to his feet. He winced and cried
But walked with me, one foot gimpy sliding

Behind him. The prison guards still left

MESSIAH   Anne Babson

Stared at us. I lifted his hand in the air
Like a boxer who has won the fight. Bereft
Of their first fruit, the guards tore their hair.
He is my other father as I have said.
He is still quite sorry for what he did.
He could not imagine any of what ended
Up. Your oldest prodigal father, friend,
And mine, is forgiven — like you, mended.

MESSIAH   Anne Babson

BEHOLD, I TELL YOU A MYSTERY

"Behold, I shew you a mystery; we shall not all sleep, but we shall all be changed, in a moment, in the twinkling of an eye, at the last trump: for the trumpet shall sound, and the dead shall be raised incorruptible, and we shall be changed." — 1 Corinthians 15:51–52

This old CD is full of digitally remastered recordings, trust me.
That old mausoleum is long-since emptied, trust me.

I unfolded the jewel case, put it in the black deck, and pressed play.
I clamped on the headphones. I could no longer breathe.

Oh, music! Oh, America! Oh, blow! Oh, blow! Oh, buss me
With that puckered mouth, with that brass daffodil!

MESSIAH   Anne Babson

AIR: THE TRUMPET SHALL SOUND

*"For the trumpet shall sound, and the dead shall be raised incorruptible, and we shall be changed." —
1 Corinthians 15:52*

When the horn blows,
We will hear the crepe of chairs scraping on the linoleum,
The bray of silver tray clattering against marble staircase, of
Ice chips chiming against the metal bar top,

And of course, the sound of Ella's crooning to us
Like a siren on the rocks, beckoning us to rise,
And we will leave our beaded bags hung on the fan backs,
Take a last sip of our cosmopolitans, and get out
Of our seats, make a beeline for the bandstand.

When the horn blows,
We will hear the scrap of the entire brass section,
The scowl of Louis' growling scat, or is it glossolalia,
We will hear the slithering of snare sticks, the plump lumping
Of the big bass, the tinkling syncopation of the piano,

And of course, the sound of one hand clapping
A finger crooked and wiggled, beckoning us to rise,
And we each will grab the waist of the nearest smoldering
Smiling one, the hand of the nearest handsome winsome one,
And shuffle out on the pressed plywood polished platform.

When the horn blows,
We will hear the slaking snake oil snake hips shake, ship–sinking
Loose lips licking, slicking, sticking, all melt into the
Maracas' mosh, the guitar's gait, the Xylophone's phone calls,
The tom–tom, tom–tom, blood and tom–tom of Gene's gongs,

And of course, the sound of the emcee's requested drum roll, please,
Suspense suspended in the clarinet's amber trills beckoning us to rise
And we will bop, strut, spin, trip the alarm, spin on the rip cord,
And lift each other up like pair skaters figuring future fractals.

When the horn blows,
We will hear the chandelier buckle under the weight of the
Fat lady singing, swinging, ring–clinging, the ballroom columns
Festooned with the tunes limpid lagooning, burning down like
Church candles, Guy's countdown to the new birth —five–four–
Three–two–one —and of course, the mirrored ball dropping like

MESSIAH
Anne Babson

A sugar cube in spumante poured out to fete our departure,
Its refraction-shooting descent above us beckoning us to rise

And when the horn blows, we will float up on its divine sonority.
A red carpet rolled out for our parade upward, the swing swung
Swimmingly by the sultan of swat, our moon-glowing big band
Blower will knock us —the melded orb of jitterbuggers ascending
On a copper-coated note held by the virtuoso for many measures —
Toward the bleachers, above the back fence and out of the park.

RECITATIVE: THEN SHALL BE BROUGHT TO PASS

"So when this corruptible shall have put on incorruption, and this mortal shall have put on immortality, then shall be brought to pass the saying that is written, Death is swallowed up in victory." — 1 Corinthians 15:54

Fortune Cookie sayings for this new day dawning:

Your great-great-great grandfather resurrected stops by to say hello.

Every pony you bet on at the track wins today and tomorrow.

Your least favorite body part is glorified. You look marvelous.

This cookie contains all the money you will ever need. See attached.

Look to your left. The person sitting there loves you.

Look to your right. The person sitting there loves you.

Ask your waiter for another glass of water. He loves you.

You love everyone. You kiss everyone. Everyone kisses you.

You never have any reason to cry or get angry. Lucky numbers: all.

This is the last fortune cookie ever. Beware of absolutely nothing.

MESSIAH   Anne Babson

BUT THANKS BE TO GOD

"But thanks be to God, which giveth us the victory through our Lord Jesus Christ." — 1 Corinthians 15:57

"And I will give unto thee…the land wherein thou art a stranger." — Genesis 17:8

But thanks be to God. One of us went first.
Someone had to trek through the underbrush,
Bearing and brandishing a two-edged
Machete to cut serpentine ferns out
                             Of the Honey Island Swamp opening
                             The path to something much wilder than that
                             Old Ponce–de–Leon–dreamed–up fountain of
                             Youth, merely youth renewed, much richer than

Candide's hidden El Dorado pursued
Passionately by conquistadors
For gold sand that passes through the hour glass,
Much more useful than the Northwest Passage,
                             Henry Hudson's conceived commuter tool
                             Elusive as a fast lane entering
                             The Holland Tunnel, and this just for speed,
                             Much more practical than the Manifest

Destiny discerned by Jefferson's men,
A papoose on Sacajawea's back,
For sinners, despite our heaviness, get
Carried across all the Rockies by Him.
                             But thanks be to God. We couldn't survive
                             The yellow fever of our own filth, all
                             We wandering Jamestowners waiting to
                             Perish in the climate of this promised

Terrain, were we bound to enter on our
Own. Someone had to offer Himself up
As meat for this Donner Party band of
Survivors. Someone had to say in this
                             Perilous place: *"I am the only right*
                             Circumnavigation, my explorers.
                             Follow me, your map, only this single
                             Cartography, to discover Vineland."

MESSIAH   Anne Babson

IF GOD BE FOR US

"What shall we then say to these things? If God be for us, who can be against us?" — *Romans 8:31–34*

The admin assist eats her lunch on the
Park bench outside the corporate complex.
She takes half a sandwich out of a white
Paper bag and nibbles it. Her boss eats
In the executive dining room, where
She is not allowed, except when she has
An urgent message for him. She munches
Her apple and decides to slip him a
Pink note, goes in under the fluorescent
Lamps, hangs up her thin winter coat, pulls out
A thick pad and scribbles back at her desk:
"URGENT – If you knew what was really in
My account upstairs, you would stand now and
Pull out a chair, invite me to join you."

MESSIAH   Anne Babson

IN THANKS FOR MARY

Her laminated face stares back from the cover of *Seventeen*,
My first fashion magazine, bought with my own money. I am
Twelve, and Her row of teeth is an escape ladder. In my sleep–walked
patrols, I wander the school hallways, palpating for seams in the
Paper–stapled walls for exits hidden behind class murals, ones that
Lead to up escalators to thirty–fourth floor apartments, balconies
overlooking rows of headlights like ants exiting the hill. I am twelve.
I have never craned my neck at a skyscraper in this two–story town.
I have only memorized the face in *Seventeen*, some staid prose from
Waiting room copies of *The New Yorker*, and my future escape route.

%

Make no mistake. What I am talking about is impossible, is lunatic!
Vegas has no odds on it, but Jehovah wove it into the paisley, this

Golden thread zigzagging the rug, not to show an imperfection, rather
That perfection itself is a sucker bet that pays off one hundred to one.

This is a true story.
You will not believe it, neither would I, but I swear on my
Mother's couplet, every word is a fabric swatch from the Great Decorator!

%

Twenty years ago, I bought the *Seventeen* at the Lucky Supermarket in
Mountain View, California, with my allowance after begging, swearing
That I was, too, I was old enough. Now I am too old for it. I am thirty–two.
I followed the face, the escape route to Manhattan like a subway connection
Tunnel, and I have a week's assignment in Rockefeller Center, over the
Forbidden rooftop gardens there and
The improbable cake spires of Saint Patrick's.
How silly to squeeze a candy jar in the middle of all these Bauhaus boxes!
At the next cubicle the woman looks familiar. She is smiling.
I know that mouth,
Every toehold of it! Years ago, she beckoned me here.
It is her, that cover girl,
Only now she is a cover woman, or
Perhaps a woman in the middle pages in
A serious article about coping with loss, a true–life model confession with
Pull–out quotes of what happens after the photo shoot. They have hauled
Away the lights on me, too, removed the Mylar reflectors.
I, too, have wiped

MESSIAH
Anne Babson

Away the heavy rouge and the absurd purple mascara and
Have waddled home
Après–club feet blistered from the heels, dress stinking of
Blended–malt scotch
And sweat, the glamor lost somewhere on the dance floor with
My other earring.
We become friends, the ex–model and the ex–pre–teen, in
The flash of a Polaroid.

%

You think you've heard it all, the whole metric conversion, you poker–faced
Sophisticates, so–called believers in so–called probability, you science slaves!

You think the lightning has struck twice, and that's the end of the story, and
You'll go home now, shrug your shoulders, call it a Houdini illusion, swear

I used mirrors, the latch wasn't really padlocked, the box really didn't go
Under the volcano before I emerged in the straight jacket and unhooked it!

You periodic table dancers, why do you insist a box step is life's fandango?
Listen, you lite rock fans, listen to the irresistible tom–tom solo and
Move your feet!

%

My week above the hanging gardens and
The flying butresses has evaporated.
Mary, that is her name, my new friend, named for
An improbable mother of miracles,
Mary, full of grace, she says to me,
"We should get together and do something
Big," as if our post–adolescent–meets–post–cover–girl encounter has not been
Big enough already to warrant a wrist–slap from all the
Reasonable people in town!
I say, laughing, "Like what? Blow up the World Trade Center?" We both
Crack up! It's ludicrous, two
New York post–divas like us, lovers of this skyline,
And somehow it sticks. It becomes our secret handshake.
We give each other
Code names, talk about the venue of our plan as
Ground Zero, and this as the
Twins loom above us impervious to us,
Two lead–lined mountains, the bulwark of
A solid economy where reasonable people commute every morning, and We,

MESSIAH
Anne Babson

Supposing our own insignificance, keep this joke, the joke of
Two unmemorable
Women of narrow escapes from immovable things, as
Our little wink and nod,
Our Wonderland Mad Hatter tea party conversation for two more years.

%

You've read the paper this morning,
Switched on the morning news show, and
Gone on the Internet, too, and you think you know the forecast here,
You think

You know how the story ends, but you're as clueless as a
Weatherman during
Global warming. You have no idea what happens next, and if
You think you do,

You are more boring than a banker's stripes by whom no one is healed. No,
Auditors. You are Brad and Janet, and this is your
Rocky Horror Picture Show,

And your car just broke down in the rain. The
Weatherman predicted clear skies.
Abandon what you wish you knew at the side of the road.
You don't know Jack.
%

I get an e–mail from Mary, whom I hail. She is *full of grace*. She LOLs me.
*"You won't believe it! Guess where I just got a job! Yes! The eighty–eighth
Floor!"* I write back, LOLing all over the World Wide Web, *"Good work!
You have infiltrated our target!"* She starts immediately.
Soon, I get another
E–mail, which I quote:
*"It's a long way down, and I have to swallow four times
On the elevator to keep my ears from popping, but the view of
Miss Lady Liberty
Is great. Please write back!
I feel far away from the world up here in my tower.
(Of course, one of the people on this e–mail list knows that my being here is
Really just part of our plot to take over). Lots of love,"*

Hail Mary, full of grace.

%

MESSIAH
Anne Babson

You heard me! I said you don't know Jack! You and all your professors,
None of them knew Dick of Dick of Tom, Dick and Harry — nada,
Eric Estrada!

You've read the actuarial reports. You've studied statistics. You've learned
How to aim a gun, and you know what happens to the tin can when you pull

The trigger. But then, one day, you and your gun club,
You arrive at the rifle
Range, and the cans, the tin cans, they strike back. Watch out!
You don't know.

%

It is September 11th, 2001. I am on my way to work in
Chelsea, the very West
Side. I am on a high floor, and nothing is between my window and Mary's.
It's a mile away, but I sometimes wave to her. Today, I arrive.
My secretary
Is sobbing. She tells me to look out the window. I see the floor where Mary works
Engulfed in smoke. I gasp, then pray an escape ladder for each of her Teeth. I pray
Her smile, not the tired one, the one on the front of
Seventeen, the light in the
Cliff tower that led me here. I pray for safety. I know.
I know knowing as only one
Who knows what she knows what she knows that this is our
Appointment, our
Reason for knowing each other, the reason
I bought the magazine when I was
Twelve when I could have bought some Bonne Bell lip gloss and nail polish
Instead.
This is why my resume was pulled out of the file at the temp agency,
Why the other worker caught the flu that week. This is why. This is why I
Work in this building, with a view of the flames, the
View of the now collapsing
Towers, the view of the fleeing people, the
View of the bright sky where there
Was solid concrete, where all the reasonable people worked, and I know.
I know like knowing was never before known. I know as I am known that
Mary, *Mary full of grace*, Mary who gets to work early and stays late, Mary,
Mary full of grace, Mary who never would have left without asking others to
Go with her, Mary, my escape route, the escape route of childhood dreams,

MESSIAH   Anne Babson

Mary, *Mary full of grace*, my Mary, my Mary cover girl, she is safe.

%

You, who are so fond of facts, let me recite a few for you:
The offices of the eighty-eighth floor were hot enough that

When the jet fuel ignited, people's glasses melted off their faces.
Doors were locked in the tower fire escapes, and thousands

Perished because managers concerned about corporate security, the
Stealing of computers, which are now dust heaps, shut them out.

Only two people on the eighty-eighth floor of the first tower that
Collapsed on September 11th, 2001, survived. One of them was

Covered with third-degree burns on seventy-seven percent of her
Flesh. They gave her the last rites as the ambulance pulled away.

One person, the other person who survived from that floor, she
Was there when the plane hit, but she got home without a scratch.

%

I heard nothing for three days. I called her company. They had
Opened a crisis hotline, where a man told me, "Hey, you never know."
I could tell he thought he knew for sure. Finally, I got the phone call:

My soul doth magnify the Lord, and my spirit hath rejoiced...
"At first, all the doors were locked. I had to go back up a flight..."

..In God My Savior; for He hath regarded the low estate of...
"And cross the floor, which was filled with smoke, to get to another..."

...His handmaiden: For, behold, from henceforth all generations....
"...Stairwell. I was able to walk down maybe ten, fifteen flights..."

...Shall call me blessed   For He that is mighty hath done...
"...Before there was another locked door. There was a crowd, waiting..."

...To me great things, and holy is His Name. And His mercy is on them...
"For the fire department to unlock it. I must have been the only one..."

that fear him from generation to generation. He hath shown the strength...
"Who saw the man who opened a door on the floor near where I stood,"

MESSIAH
Anne Babson

...Of His arm;
He hath scattered the proud in the imagination of their hearts.
"A man in a suit, very calm, smiling at me. He said he knew a way out,"

He hath put down the mighty from their seats, and
Exalted them of low degree.
"That I should come with him. I was the only one who followed, and..."

He hath filled the hungry with good things, and the
Rich he hath sent empty away.
"...He led me to a stairwell which was open all the way down. I turned..."

He hath helped His servant Israel, in remembrance of His mercy; as He
"To thank him, but he was gone. I walked outside, and when I was about...'

Spake to our fathers, to Abraham, and to His seed...
"A block away, the building fell, but even though people died around me,"
...Forever.
"All around me, nothing hit me. I don't have a cut or a bruise. I'm okay."

%

I dare you. I double-dog dare you not to talk yourself out of this blessing!
Go run that into your spread sheet and tell me how many zeros you get!

You will reason your way out of this by lunch time. You will tell yourself
I exaggerated. I am a poet, and poets use hyperbole. You will laugh

At yourself for this passing pause. You will go back to your
Monkey-evolved scratching and picking, and you will forget me,

But do not forget Mary. Do not forget her. I will find you and cut you
If you forget the woman who rescued me from Mountain View by

Smiling. I will track down your zombie office and chain myself
To your waiting room table if you call anything dumb about her luck.

From the grave, I will haunt you, you who read this generations from now,
If you doubt me. I will know. I will make you realize that all odds are odd.

Now and forever, all bets are off. Behold the Hand of the Almighty, who
Rescues all those who keep the appointments He sets, who crack His jokes.

MESSIAH   Anne Babson

WORTHY IS THE LAMB THAT WAS SLAIN

"And every creature which is in heaven, and on the earth, and under the earth, and such as are in the sea, and all that are in them, heard I saying, Blessing, and honor, and glory, and power." — *Revelation 5:12–13*

Thus, we see that true power
Is not expressed through display of great riches
But by kneeling down, washing feet. Wisdom
Cries in some streets, but shows her strongest strength
Quietly. To be honored, give honor,
Sow into the ground and the sky glory,

Humbling one's self to one's work is glory.
Leadership looks like elbow grease, power
Like compromise. To breathe is an honor
For which the honored owe thanks. Great riches
Are housed in the O2 molecules; strength
Emanates from them. Thus declares Wisdom,

Adjusting her bifocals, that all wisdom
And might come to all who survive, glory
To the Great Rescuer of us all, strength
To all who survive, too, if they just power
Their way to these qualities through riches
Given away, honor to dishonored

And unsung daily–grind heroes, honor
Given to the groundlings. Reasons Wisdom,
Like Dolly in that musical, *"Riches*
Are like dung. To bloom in their full glory,
They must be buried first to rise power–wielding."
Therefore in the tomb, only strength

Of our Great Escape Artist, only strength
In His grave–going for us, just honor
In His stripe–streaking for us, just power
In His helplessness for us, says Wisdom.
See the limits of your own vainglory
The way you see the limits of riches

You can earn alone. The truest riches
Accrue above, costing nothing. True strength
Muscles above, not in our arms, glory
Mantles above us around the Honored

MESSIAH   Anne Babson

One, not around our shoulders. True wisdom
Wisely puts limits on reason's power

To instruct us how to live.
Live Gloriously! Live Honorably!
Live Richly! Live Wisely!
Live powerfully, strongly kneeling, singing!

MESSIAH   Anne Babson

AMEN

Thank you so much,
Uptown Planet Earth, for your warm reception this evening.
It has been a pleasure to play for you.

I'd like to introduce you to the band.

On keyboards and castanets, trained in the
Art of colonial lace making by
Wheeling, West Virginia's best tatters, give
It up for Herodotus and Hagar!

On bass and marimba, straight out of the
Miami's organ donor district, let's
 Hear it for the Archangel Gabriel
And our own Francis of Assisi!

On drums, the awesome Mr. Gene Krupa!
On oboe, clarinet, and harpsichord,
The incomparable, and elegant,
And presidential Thomas Jefferson!

On back–up vocals and prophetic words,
Please put your hands together for the great
Marvin Gaye, Woodie Guthrie,
Harriet Beecher Stowe, Pink, and Rosemary Clooney!

On harp and percussion, our favorite
New immigrant to the United States,
Please show your love for the real
Italian Stallion, Mister Dante Alighieri!

On electric guitar and a few well–
Chosen vroom–vrooms of the motorcycle
Engine, anti–satanic mechanic,
Asia's own Doctor David Yonggi Cho!

On trombone and kitchen patrol, trained in
The craft of quilt making by the poet
Lucille Clifton, please give a hand for the
Lovely and delicious Bootsie Collins!

On trumpet, Mister Louis Armstrong, as

MESSIAH   Anne Babson

If you didn't already know that, folks!
On violin and cello, please show your
Great respect for Hildegarde Von Bingen!

On saxophone and oration,
Former President Bill Clinton and much–loved,
Much–missed and still–much–needed at this hour,
Our Doctor Martin Luther King Junior!

Our fabulous Messiah oratorio dancers,
Abraham, Iassac, Jacob, Joseph, Saul, Samuel,
David, Sarah, Rahab, Eve, Abigail, Isaiah, Jeremiah!

And I am your mistress of ceremonies this evening.
I am a shadow who hopes not to have offended, like
Puck at the end of that marvelous
Fantasy about something much less important.
I am the voice of the wind that blows from
West to East across North America. I am the
Voice between commercials on your television, that old
High hum under that test pattern
You saw when networks went off air.
I am the
Emergency Broadcast System.
This has been so much more than a test.

This has been an emergency.
This has been the day you hear about yourself from your best
Friend who is not just flattering you.
This has been the day you hear about your future,
At least your potential future,
From the mouth of the faucet as you wash your face.
After you hear this voice,
You usually tell yourself you were imagining things.
Don't tell yourself
That now.
Tell yourself instead that you were having a vision, a
Paginated
Vision, but still
A vision, like Jacob's ladder, like sheaves bowing to
Joseph, a vision that is truth without being journalism.

Don't shake it off, out the door in uniform already having forgotten.
Those trumpets blared in shofar revile.
Note the pause before the recorded voice.

MESSIAH   Anne Babson

You have had a vision. This is the
Emergency Broadcast System
Your mind picks up when the television is off.
Stay tuned for updates.

Amen.

ACKNOWLEDGMENTS

Flying buttresses supporting this book — The Corporation of Yaddo and Vermont Studio Center where I resided while writing it, Agi Fodor, a lifelong friend who was kind enough to take me to Lincoln Center to the "do it yourself" Messiah where I got the idea for it, Marilyn Hacker, my great mentor who is gracious and intelligent enough not to expect poets who sit under her tutelage to turn into her clones, only excellent writers, Cornelius Eady, Richard Tayson, Linsey Abrams, and others who have been kind enough to encourage me along the way, Su Lian Tan, composer and co-conspirator, and Katharine, a school teacher in Saratoga Springs who was so inspired by the idea of this project that she fasted and prayed for me one day a month while I wrote it.

Several of these poems were featured in spoken word form on the compilation holy hip-hop CD *The Cornerstone* (2007, New Lew Music)
"And He Shall Purify" and "Behold, A Virgin Shall Conceive" appeared in *14 Magazine* in the UK.
"Every Valley Shall Be Exalted" appeared in *The Ampersand Review*.
"In Thanks for Mary" was featured on *The Arnie Arneson Show* and was turned into a one-woman show by actress Maria Brooks, performing at The Montauk Club in 2004.
"But Thanks Be To God" appeared in *Backlash* in the UK.
"Surely He Hath Borne Our Griefs" appeared in *Bible Advocate* in the USA and in Latin America.
"Behold and See if There Be Any Sorrow" appeared in *Blossombones*.
"The People that Walked in Darkness" appeared in *Cantaraville*.
"Recitative: Then Shall Be Brought to Pass" appeared in *The Christian Century*.
"Thy Rebuke Hath Broken His Heart" appeared in *Current Accounts* in the UK.
"Let Us Break Their Bonds Assunder" and "Their Sound is Gone Out" appeared in *The Denver Syntax*.
"Then Shall the Eyes of the Blind" appeared in the British Anthology *Emergency Verse* (Caparison Books, 2011, UK).
"Recitative: Unto Which of the Angels Said He at Any Time" appeared in *Forge*.
"The Rich Young Ruler" appeared in *Friends Journal*.
"Thus Saith the Lord (Transposed for Soprano)" appeared in *Language and Culture*.
"Recitative: Thus Saith the Lord" appeared in *Liturgical Credo*.
"Air: The Trumpet Shall Sound" appeared in *National Poetry Review*.
"Since by Man Came Death" appeared in *The Neovictorian*.
"He was Cut Off" appeared in *Not One of Us*.
"And the Glory of the Lord: Legato Arrangement" appeared in *Lotus Eater Literary Magazine* in Italy.
"All They That See Him Laugh Him to Scorn" and "He Trusted in God" appeared in *Offcourse Literary Journal*.

"Chorus: Glory to God" appeared in a philosophical writings anthology entitled *Paradoxism*.

"Darkness Shall Cover the Earth" appeared in *Pennsylvania Literary Journal*.

"And With His Stripes We Are Healed" and "O Death Where Is Thy Sting" appeared in *The Penwood Review*.

"But Who" appeared in *Poem*.

"From a Scroll Found at Nag Haamadi" appeared in *Poetica: A Journal of Jewish Thought*.

"Pifa (Pastoral Symphony)" appeared in *River Oak Review*.

"His Yoke Is Easy" appeared in *Saint Katherine Journal*.

"Recitative: Behold, I Tell You a Mystery" and "Rejoice Greatly" appeared in *Second Nature Journal*.

"Chorus: Let All the Angels of God Worship Him" appeared in *Soul Lit*.

"Chorus: Hallelujah" appeared in *The Spoon River Poetry Review* and won its editor's award.

"Air: But Thou Didst Not Leave His Soul in Hell" appeared in *T.J. Eckleberg Review*.

"He was Despised" appeared in *Tuck Magazine*.

Thank you for the general encouragement of the Peauxdunque Writers Association, a clandestine society shrouded in holy mysteries, whose members have plied me with drink and have generally encouraged my behavior.

I would also especially like to thank my husband, Chuck, for sustaining me in all my efforts.

NOTES

The titles of some poems refer to Handel's oratorio's choral music in the Messiah oratorio. Therefore, they are written in high-church Anglican English. There are other titles which refer to "gnostic" passages conceived by the author for artistic purposes. All passages of the Bible are quoted from the King James Version. As most sacred works of art are set in places and times contemporary to the artist, this book is at least as much a commentary on America and American music as it is any kind of exegesis.

ABOUT THE AUTHOR

Anne Babson's collection *The White Trash Pantheon* won the Colby H. Kullman prize. Her collection *Polite Occasions* was featured at the 2018 Louisiana Book Festival. She wrote the libretto for the opera *Lotus Lives*, which has been performed in multiple cities in the United States and Canada. Her play about gun culture in the South, *Reenactment*, was published by *Review Americana*. She is the author of four chapbooks — the latest of which, *Dolly Shot*, was published by Dancing Girl Press. She has been anthologized in the United States and in England, most recently in the notable collection *Nasty Women Poets: An Unapologetic Anthology of Subversive Verse*. Her work has appeared in literary journals on five continents and has won numerous editorial awards. She has been nominated for the Pushcart Prize four times. She has received residency grants from Yaddo and Vermont Studio Center. She writes and lives in New Orleans.

Visit her Amazon author page at: *https://www.amazon.com/Anne-Babson/e/B00XLAEN1I/*.

And her web site: *http://www.annebabson.com*.

Typefaces Used

BASKERVILLE – Baskerville
BOOK ANTIQUA - Book Antiqua
GARAMOND – Garamond
PERPETUA TILTING MT

www.ingramcontent.com/pod-product-compliance
Lightning Source LLC
Chambersburg PA
CBHW050455110426
42743CB00017B/3370